FAMILY LIFE IN

Ancient Greece

DR ANNE MILLARD

HODDER
Wayland

an imprint of Hodder Children's Books

FAMILY LIFE SERIES:

Ancient Egypt
Ancient Greece
Medieval Britain
Roman Britain
Saxon Britain
Second World War
Tudors & Stuarts
Victorian Britain

Series design: Pardoe Blacker Ltd
Editor: Katie Orchard
Production controller: Carol Stevens

**First published in 1995 by Wayland (Publishers) Ltd
This edition published in 2001 by Hodder Wayland,
an imprint of Hodder Children's Books
© Hodder Wayland 1995**

British Library Cataloguing in Publication Data
Millard, Anne
 Family Life in Ancient Greece. – (Family Life series)
   I. Title II. Series
   306.850938

ISBN 0 7502 3520 9

Printed and bound by G. Canale & C. S.p.A. Turin, Italy

Cover pictures: A painting on a vase showing preparations for a wedding; a doll and a baby's bottle.

Picture acknowledgements: Lesley and Roy Adkins 27 (top), 28 (top); Archiv für Kunst und Geschichte 23 (top) British Museum; Bridgeman Art Library 15 Vatican Museums and Galleries, Rome; C M Dixon 6 British Museum, 10 (left and right) both British Museum, 12 (top), 14 (top and bottom), 16 (top and bottom), 18, 21 National Museum, Athens, 24 (top) National Museum, Athens; Robert Harding 4 British Museum; Michael Holford *cover*, 7 (top and bottom) British Museum, 8 British Museum, 9 (left and right) both British Museum, 11 British Museum, 12-13 (bottom) British Museum, 13 British Museum, 17, 19 British Museum, 20, 23 (bottom), 25 British Museum, 27 (bottom) British Museum, 28 (bottom) British Museum; Zefa 22. Artwork: Nick Hawken 5, 8 (top), 24 (bottom); Peter Bull 26, 29.

CONTENTS

LIFE IN GREECE

For nearly a thousand years, from about 2000 BC, Greece had been an important power in the ancient world. This is called the **Mycenaean** Period, after the leading kingdom of Mycenae. However, the Greek kingdoms collapsed in wars and **famine**. Many people died and those who survived had to struggle just to live. Much of their time was taken up with growing enough for their families to eat. Family life for most people centred around work on the farm. They even lost the art of writing. Historians call these sad times the 'Dark Ages' of Greece. However, things began to improve.

A NEW BEGINNING

Life started to get better by about 800 BC. The economy improved and families enjoyed a higher standard of living as international trade grew. They invented a new, simple form of writing, and they lived under completely different rules from their ancestors. Greece was now divided up into a number of **city states**. Some states were very small. Athens was the largest, with only 2,500 square kilometres. At the centre of each city there was usually an **acropolis**, where the Greeks built a temple dedicated to the city's patron god or goddess.

Greek farmers' most important crops were grain for bread, grapes for wine and olives. This scene on a vase from the Archaic Period (about 800–500 BC) shows olives being harvested to make oil.

Unlike during the Mycenaean Period, most new city states did not have kings. Sparta was the exception, having two kings who ruled together. By about 800 BC, other states had a new form of government called an **oligarchy**. This meant that the city was run by a small group of **aristocrats**. As time passed, middle-class men – merchants, bankers and craftsmen – prospered and demanded a say in the running of their cities.

Naturally, the leaders did not want to give up their power and there were riots and murders. By about 650 BC, many people were so fed up with the troubles that they were prepared to have one strong man take over the running of their city and sort the problems out. This man was called a **tyrant**. Eventually, however, people became unhappy with the tyrants as well.

The early history of the new Greek states is called the Archaic Period and it lasted from about 800–500 BC.

A reconstuction of the Acropolis of Athens during the Classical Period. The Classical Period, which followed after the Archaic Period was a time of peace and prosperity in ancient Greece.

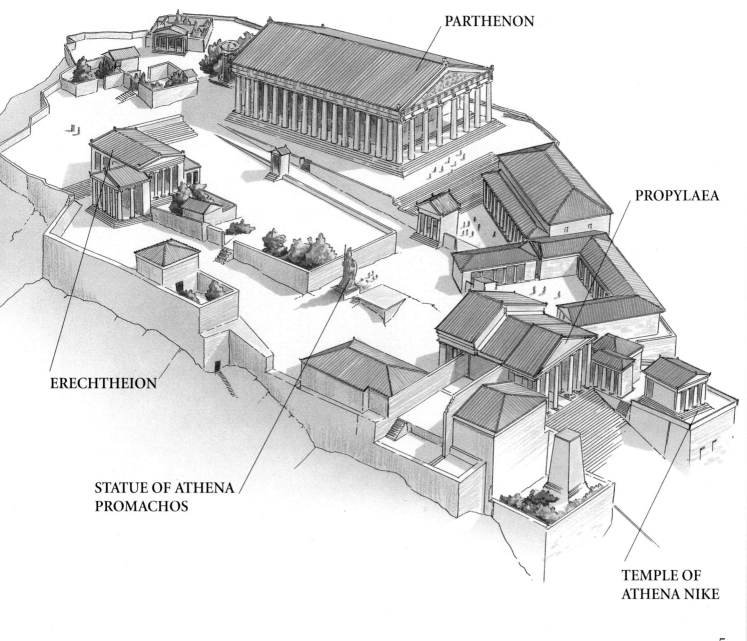

PARTHENON

PROPYLAEA

ERECHTHEION

STATUE OF ATHENA PROMACHOS

TEMPLE OF ATHENA NIKE

THE CLASSICAL PERIOD

*'The **barbarians** are slaves: we **Hellenes** are free men.'*

In 508 BC, Athens introduced a new system of law called **democracy**, which was adopted by several other city states. However, ancient Greek democracy was not as democratic as our system is today. Take Athens, for example. At the height of its power, about 250,000 people lived in Athens and the countryside around the city, but only a few thousand could take part in the government of the city. This was because to become a citizen, an ancient Greek had to be a man, come from a family native to the city, and be free born (not a slave). This did not leave many people who could vote!

Hunting provided both sport and food. This man and his dog have bagged a fox and a hare.

Women were not allowed to play any part in running the state. Foreigners who settled and worked in the city had to pay taxes and serve in the army, but did not count as citizens and therefore could not vote. Slaves – and there were many – had no rights at all. Slaves could be Greeks who had been captured in wars between the cities, or foreigners bought from slave traders. If a Greek owned a slave who was a talented craftsman, he or she would set the slave up in business and take most of the profits, but allow the slave to keep some. Such slaves could, eventually, buy their freedom but they could never be Greek citizens.

Sparta was different from the other Greek states. In about 740–720 BC, the Spartans had conquered their neighbours, the Messenians. A revolt by the Messenians had convinced the Spartans that they had to organize themselves so that they could deal with any future revolt or invasion. The Spartans became obsessed with security and military strength. Only native, free-born Spartans had any political rights and the men all had to be soldiers. The main role of women was to produce children to become soldiers. Spartan mothers also felt that if their sons went to war they must only come back victorious or dead. To run away would be a disgrace:

'Come back with your shield – or on it'.

The period from about 500–336 BC is called the Classical Period. This was when Greek civilization was at its height.

*Pericles (about 495–429 BC) was elected as a military commander or **strategos** so many times that he virtually ruled Athens for twenty years.*

(Right) A Spartan girl athlete. Girls in Sparta were encouraged to exercise so that they would be strong mothers and produce healthy children.

LIFE AT HOME

In ancient Greece, the home tended to be where women and children spent most of their time. Greek men were very rarely at home.

This reconstruction shows what a good Greek town house would have looked like. It is based on houses excavated in the city of Olynthos.

GYNAECEUM,
BEDROOMS AND SLAVES'
QUARTERS (UPSTAIRS)

KITCHEN

ANDRON
(MOSAIC FLOOR)

ANTEROOM
(MOSAIC FLOOR)

COBBLED
COURTYARD

FAMILY ALTAR

HOUSES

Greek houses were usually built of mud-bricks covered in plaster, and they had roofs made from pottery tiles. Outside, they were plain with few windows. The house overlooked and opened on to a courtyard. The family altar was in the courtyard and a rich family would have its own well. Wooden stairs led from the courtyard up to a balcony from which the rooms on the first floor could be reached. On the ground floor there would be a kitchen, an **andron** (dining room) and a room with a

A baby's feeding bottle made of pottery. A teat of cloth or leather would be fitted to the bottle for the baby to drink through.

fireplace, where the family could sit together. Some houses also had a bathroom. Upstairs was the women's room (the **gynaeceum**), bedrooms, and perhaps slave quarters. Poor families had only one or two rooms to live in and would have had to get their fresh water from the fountain house.

The chair on this vase would have a hole in the seat and a potty underneath. The baby is happily playing with a rattle.

CHILDHOOD

When a baby was born it had to be accepted by its father to be allowed to live. If it was sickly, or if the father disapproved of it, he could reject it and the poor baby would then be left outside somewhere to die.

If the baby was accepted, but was a girl, she would face a very hard life. Girls were thought to be of little value, and they were never allowed control of their lives. They always had to obey the wishes of men – fathers, brothers, husbands or sons.

Whether the child was a boy or a girl, there would be celebrations and gifts on the seventh day of its life. The child was named on the tenth day.

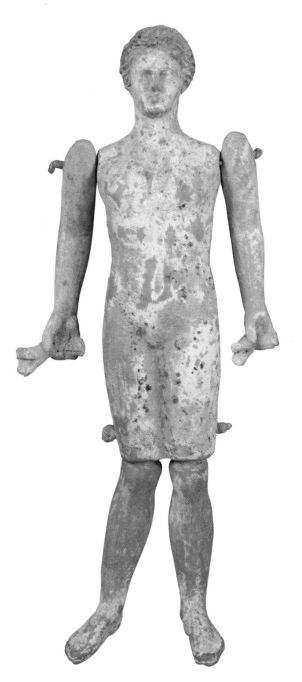

A little girl's beloved doll. Its arms and legs move.

9

EDUCATION

Girls were brought up to be good wives and mothers. If they had any education, it would be from their mothers at home. Boys, however, went to school when they were seven years old, unless their parents were too poor to pay the fees. A rich man would have a special slave to take his son to school and keep an eye on his behaviour there.

These figures show two girls playing knucklebones – a game similar to 'jacks' which was very popular with the ancient Greeks.

Besides reading, writing and arithmetic, Greek children learned music and poetry. Physical education (dancing and athletics) was believed to be very important. Boys had to grow up to be fit men, so that they could fight for their city. A boy could stay at school until he was eighteen years old, but many left earlier to start work. At eighteen, however, all young men had to do military training.

Sparta was different from the rest of ancient Greece. At seven years old, boys were taken from their home and made to live in barracks, under fierce discipline, training to be loyal and brave soldiers. Girls were trained as well – women taught them dancing and athletics. They had to become tough, healthy mothers to produce more brave soldiers.

Besides their toys, Greek children had pets to play with.

MARRIAGE

It was the duty of every Greek citizen to marry and have sons to work and fight for their city. Girls were usually married off by their fathers when they were about fifteen years old. They could not choose their own husbands and their families often chose husbands many years older than the girls. On the day before her wedding, the bride had to sacrifice all her toys. This was a sign that her childhood was over!

A young bride, preparing for her wedding.

As a wife, the girl was completely under the control of her husband, and she had to perform many duties. If her husband was poor, she had to do all the housework, such as cooking and cleaning, without any of today's modern gadgets or running water. She also had to weave cloth for clothes and for use in the house – items such as bedclothes, towels and wall hangings. If her husband was rich, she had to run the household, keeping the store-room stocked with food and wine and taking charge of the servants and slaves. She also had to raise the children, nurse sick people in the house and manage the family finances.

(Above) This figurine shows a housewife with her kitchen equipment cooking a meal. In a poor family this might have been bread or porridge with fruit, cheese or vegetables and sometimes fish. Only the rich ate meat regularly. For many, meat was a treat reserved for special occasions such as festivals.

Greek women fetching water from a public fountain. They would have to make many trips to meet their families' needs every day. Wealthy families had their own wells.

In poor Greek families, women had a chance to get out a little in the course of their busy lives, because there was no one else to do the shopping. In wealthy families, however, women hardly left the house, except for religious festivals or family celebrations. At best they managed to visit friends and hold all-women dinner parties. We would find the wealthy ancient Greek woman's life terribly limited and boring today.

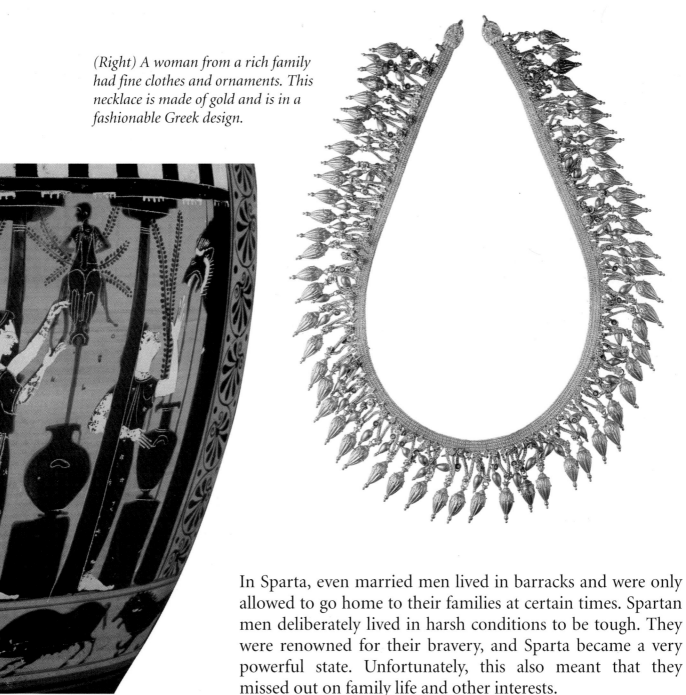

(Right) A woman from a rich family had fine clothes and ornaments. This necklace is made of gold and is in a fashionable Greek design.

In Sparta, even married men lived in barracks and were only allowed to go home to their families at certain times. Spartan men deliberately lived in harsh conditions to be tough. They were renowned for their bravery, and Sparta became a very powerful state. Unfortunately, this also meant that they missed out on family life and other interests.

(Above) This Roman mosaic shows the philosopher Plato (c.427–347 BC) teaching pupils at the school he founded called the Academy.

Men in ancient Greece were very much concerned with politics, and protecting the way of life in their towns or villages. They had little to do with the running of the home, although they were often responsible for buying the shopping.

PHILOSOPHERS AND HIGHER EDUCATION

If a boy's father was a farmer or a craftsman, the boy would probably start work young, even before he had done his military training. Rich men's sons would go on to some form of higher education. Many would study the art of public speaking so that they could become actively involved with the government of the city.

The Greek city states produced some scholars called philosophers ('which means lovers of knowledge'). These men wanted to know all about the world and how it worked. They asked questions, studied, investigated and conducted experiments in many subjects – biology and botany, maths, history, geography and astronomy. They also studied people – how they behaved, why they did things and what the best system of government might be. Socrates, Plato and Aristotle were some of these philosophers. Young men flocked to listen to them, to discuss and to learn. It was a little like a university today.

LEISURE

Greek men lived much of their lives separate from their wives and children. They were involved in politics and business, and spent much of their spare time away from the house. Their idea of a party was to invite other men to dinner. No women were invited, except as hired entertainers. Music, poetry, wine and lively discussion made it a good party.

BEING A GOOD CITIZEN

'Man is a political animal'.

All citizens were expected to play an active role in the running of their city. In Athens, for example, there was an Assembly which met every ten days. Every citizen could attend, speak and vote on new laws proposed by the Council. The members of the Council, who ran the state, were citizens chosen randomly each year. Other government officials were also voted for each year to enforce the laws and run the state.

The Greeks loved board games. The picture on this vase shows the great heroes, Ajax and Achilles, absorbed in play.

(Left) Socrates (c.469–399 BC), the most famous of all Greek philosophers.

There were also important leaders called strategoi, who were elected each year. They could be re-elected as many times as people voted for them, but being a politician in Athens could cause real trouble. If a politician's fellow citizens did not like his ideas, they could vote to exile him (send him away) for ten years.

There were no lawyers in Greece to present citizens' cases, so they had to present their own. Foreigners (even if they were from another Greek state), were not allowed to speak in court, so they had to ask a local citizen to explain their cases for them. Jurymen were chosen randomly and were paid, since they were unable to earn money while they were in court.

(Above) A carpenter saws a plank of wood. Perhaps he is going to make a beautiful chest, couch or table – the main items of furniture in a Greek house.

One of Greece's many talented metal-workers, hard at work at his forge.

In Sparta there was no democracy, and even true Spartans only had limited political power. Non-Spartans were thought to be inferior and had no rights at all. Most non-Spartans were helots, or peasants, who were little better-off than slaves. They had to give most of their crops to their Spartan masters, leaving them free to be full-time soldiers. A few were craftspeople and traders who lived in separate villages. They were called **perioiloi**.

This bronze helmet was captured by the men of Argos in a war against Corinth. They dedicated it to the god Zeus.

MILITARY SERVICE AND INTER-CITY WARS

As in Sparta, all citizens of the other Greek states were expected to train as soldiers. Between the ages of twenty and fifty, citizens had to be prepared to fight for their city whenever it went to war, so the men would often be away from their families during this time. Most Greek soldiers were **hoplites** (foot soldiers). A group of hoplites was called a **phalanx**, which attacked and moved together. Only small numbers of mounted warriors were used until around 334 BC.

Sadly, wars between city states were very common. Battles raged, crops were ruined, and cities were surrounded and attacked. Families were often destroyed as fathers and husbands were killed.

RELIGIOUS LIFE

Religion played a very important part in the family lives of the ancient Greeks. In the courtyard of a Greek house there was an altar where the family could make offerings to the gods. Many houses also had a special room, where a fire burned in honour of the family goddess Hestia. In many families, prayers and offerings would be made every day and all family festivals, such as name days and weddings, were held at home.

A young woman makes an offering at an altar. Women had an important role in the religious life of their families. Usually, the women made regular offerings at the tombs of dead family members and tended the family altar. The father would lead the family prayers.

THE DEITIES

The Greeks honoured twelve great deities (gods and goddesses), and many lesser ones. The great gods were Zeus (King of the gods), Poseidon (lord of the seas), Pluto (ruler of the Underworld), Ares (the god of war), Hermes (the messenger of the gods) and Apollo (god of the sun, music and poetry). The six great goddesses were Hera (sister-wife of Zeus, who protected women and marriage), Hestia (who cared for the home and the family), Demeter (who made the land fertile), Aphrodite (goddess of love and beauty), Artemis (goddess of the moon and hunting) and Athene (goddess of wisdom and war). The Greeks had many stories about the gods and how they were involved in people's lives.

MESSAGES FROM THE GODS

The Greeks believed that their gods sent them messages called oracles. Under very special conditions, the gods would inspire certain priestesses to speak for them. The gods also sent omens, or warnings, to the Greeks, by such things as thunder and the flight of birds.

TEMPLES

Every city had beautiful temples dedicated to the great gods and goddesses, and to many of the lesser ones as well. A temple was usually built on a platform so people went up steps to get into it. Inside, there was a large room containing a statue of the god or goddess to whom it was dedicated. Behind this was a smaller room called a cella, where they stored the offerings of gold, silver and bronze made to the temple.

Aphrodite, goddess of love and beauty. This statue was made during the Hellenistic Period (between 200–100 BC) and was found in eastern Turkey.

People could go to a temple to offer private prayers. Sometimes they would ask the gods for a special favour. Outside a temple was an altar, where official offerings were made and animals were sacrificed. At all the great state festivals, magnificent processions would wind their way through the city to a temple altar to offer sacrifices.

Some people did not find the ordinary Greek religion satisfying, so they joined special religious groups called 'mystery cults' and they had to promise never to reveal the secrets they would learn. They had to study hard to pass all the tests in order to become proper members, who knew all the secrets.

The once magnificent temple of Apollo at Delphi is now a ruin. Here, Apollo's priestess gave messages or oracles in his name.

A typical decorated tombstone. A tombstone would often show the dead person with a close family member. This one shows a man and his son.

When people died, there would be a funeral procession with guests weeping loudly. The deceased were either buried, or cremated (burned) and their ashes were buried. Food, drink and personal possessions were put in the tomb and a monument was built over it, where offerings would later be made.

Greeks believed their souls were ferried across the River Styx (the river of death) by an old ferryman called Charon. A coin had to be buried with the dead person to pay him. The souls of the dead people then passed through the gate to the Underworld. This was guarded by a three-headed dog called Cerberus, who made sure none of Pluto's subjects escaped! In the Underworld, the souls were judged. Very wicked souls were taken to Tartarus, where they were punished for eternity. Very good souls were rewarded by going to a beautiful place called the Elysian Fields. Most souls did not fall into either of these groups, as they were not entirely good or bad. They had to spend eternity wandering in the Asphodel Fields, a grey, boring place. Only when a relative made offerings to them would they briefly feel alive again. That was why it was so important for a family to make regular offerings to loved ones who had died.

LIFE IN A CITY

A view over the ruins of the agora in Athens as it looks today.

City life was always bustling with people, noise, and money changing hands. There were plenty of shops, markets and entertainment, such as the latest play being performed.

SHOPS AND MARKETS

There were small shops and workshops scattered across every Greek city. A typical workshop would be run by a craftsman, one or two assistants (perhaps his son and a hired workman) and a slave or two. There they would produce the objects that are now admired in museums all over the world. At the heart of each city was the **agora**. This was a bustling, noisy place where stalls were set up and country people and fishermen offered their goods for sale. There were stalls for other goods too, where shoppers could buy everything from sandals to slaves. People could also hire servants. For example, they might not be able to afford to employ a skilled chef all the time, but they could hire one for a night for a special dinner-party.

Bankers and money-changers had tables where people could borrow money, or invest their savings. Foreigners would come to change their money into the coins of the city.

A Greek coin made of silver. Coins were first made in Lydia (a kingdom in what is now Turkey) in the seventh century BC. The Greeks soon adopted the idea.

The stoa built by Attalus (159–138 BC), King of Pergamum, around the main market-place in Athens. It has been reconstructed to show how it looked in the days of its glory.

Although peasant women might be found selling food at some stalls, and women of the poorer classes might be found doing the shopping, in many families, men or slaves usually bought the food. The women stayed at home.

Around the agora was the **stoa**, a line of columns holding up a roof, where friends met to gossip and philosophers walked and taught their pupils. This area shaded the fronts of shops where expensive goods could be bought – gold jewellery, spices, and luxury cloth like rare silk. The stoa buildings were also a popular place to set up barbers' shops, schools and doctors' surgeries.

Actors, carrying their masks, make an offering to their patron Dionysus (the god of wine).

Everywhere a Greek person walked in the city, he or she would see beautiful temples and public buildings, built from marble with red tiles on the roofs. There were fine paintings that decorated the walls of the stoa, and statues in public places of gods and goddesses, heroes, politicians and successful athletes. Greek sculptors were very skilled at making life-like human figures.

A reconstruction of a Greek theatre. Plays were only performed on a few special days a year as part of religious festivals. Prices were very low and almost everyone could afford to see the plays, so theatres were usually very large.

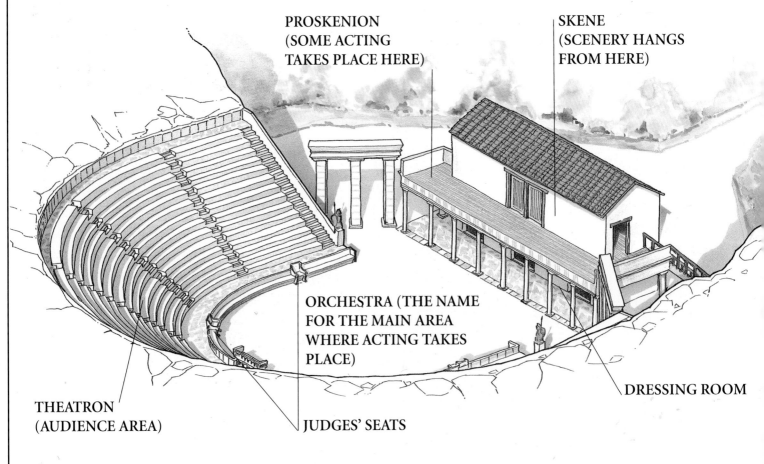

PROSKENION (SOME ACTING TAKES PLACE HERE)

SKENE (SCENERY HANGS FROM HERE)

ORCHESTRA (THE NAME FOR THE MAIN AREA WHERE ACTING TAKES PLACE)

DRESSING ROOM

THEATRON (AUDIENCE AREA)

JUDGES' SEATS

24

Greek cities would have open-air theatres where people could see plays by great writers such as Aeschylus, Euripides and Sophocles. Plays started off as hymns in honour of the gods and these hymns developed into plays with several characters and a chorus (who helped the action along by making comments and asking questions). All the parts, even those of women, were played by men wearing masks. Competitions for new plays were held as part of major religious festivals.

Boy jockeys encourage their horses in a race. This vase was itself once awarded to the winner of a race at a long-passed Olympic Games.

THE GAMES

Athletic contests were also held during religious festivals in every city, but there were four contests, or Games, that were famous internationally – the Olympic, Pythian, Ishmian and Nemean Games. The Olympic Games started in 776 BC and were held every four years. People came from all over Greece and its **colonies** to compete in them. All wars had to stop, to give the athletes and spectators the chance to get there. Travelling overland in Greece was very difficult anyway, because of the mountains. There was no public transport and few roads. Whenever possible, people preferred to go by sea, at least for part of the journey. The events at these Games were running, boxing, wrestling, the **pentathlon** (five athletic events), horse racing and chariot racing.

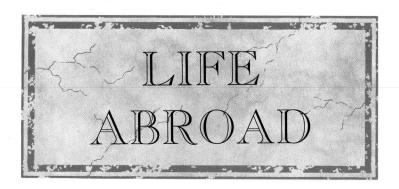

LIFE ABROAD

By about 800 BC, the population of Greece was growing so quickly that there was not enough land to go round. Some families decided they must seek new homes and a new life abroad. For about 150 years, families left Greece and settled round the eastern Mediterranean, in southern Italy and in the south of France. The area along the western coast of what is now Turkey was called Ionia, and many Greek colonies were founded there.

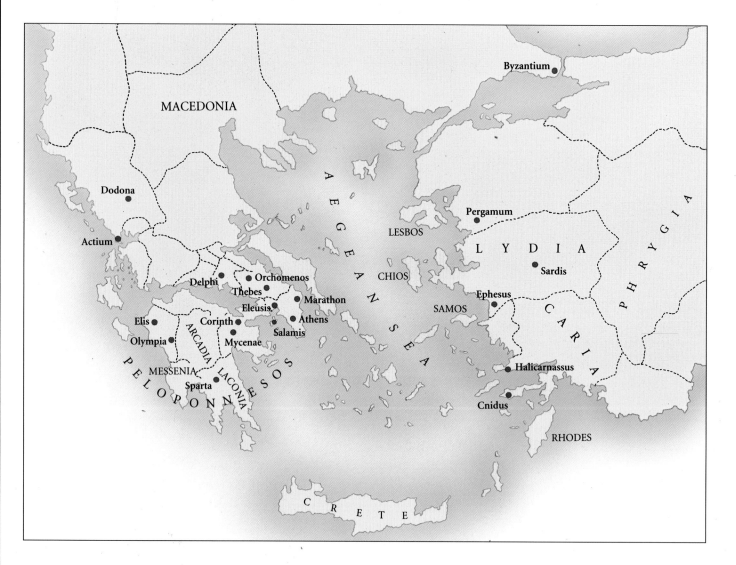

This map shows the main cities of Greece and its colonies in Ionia (the coast of modern Turkey).

COLONISTS

Once settled, the colonists became farmers, founded new cities and introduced the Greek way of life to the areas that they settled in. The colonists had special trading relationships with the cities they had left in Greece and they became the leading traders there. Besides their colonies, they had trading posts in other places too. In Egypt, for example, Greek colonists were given the city of Daphnae as their trading base.

The colonists' sailing ships, crammed with all sorts of goods, stayed close to the coasts where possible, going across the open sea only when necessary. They tried to avoid sailing during the winter gales but even so, some ships and their crews were lost. Underwater archaeologists have discovered several of these ancient Greek shipwrecks, so we are learning a lot about how these ships were made and what they carried.

Taking their architecture and religion with them, Greek colonists in Paestum (in southern Italy) built this impressive temple to their goddess Hera.

This heavily-laden Greek merchant sailing ship is about to be rammed by a war-galley, which is being rowed towards it.

*A Roman **mosaic** showing Alexander the Great at the Battle of Issus in 333 BC, chasing the fleeing Persian King Darius III.*

*An example of the art of the Hellenistic Period. This bronze head of a **Berber** was found in the temple of Apollo, built by Greek colonists in Cyrene, on the north African coast.*

MERCENARIES

Some adventurous young Greek men decided not to move abroad permanently, but to find work as soldiers with foreign princes. The reputation of the Greek hoplites was so good that many Middle Eastern monarchs, including the pharaohs of Egypt, were eager to hire them as **mercenaries**.

THE PERSIAN MENACE

The Greeks' most bitter enemies were the Persians, whose mighty empire stretched from the borders of India in the east, across to the shores of the Mediterranean in the west, and included Egypt as well. The Greek colonists of Ionia were among its subjects. The mainland Greeks openly supported the colonists, which angered the Persian kings.

The Persians invaded Greece twice, so Greek children were brought up to believe that the Persians were evil. These invasions affected family life in Greece a great deal. People were taxed heavily to pay for the wars. Also, many men died, leaving the wives to bring up their families alone.

Darius I led the first invasion of Greece, in 490 BC. The Greeks' bravery and wisdom helped them defeat the Persians.

In 480 BC, Xerxes led the huge Persian army back to Greece. Outnumbered once more, with Athens left burning and in ruins, everything looked hopeless for the Greeks until they used their secret weapon – a huge fleet of fast, sleek warships called triremes. The Persians were defeated and driven off. Athenian men and boys believed that rowers on these ships were as heroic as soldiers.

THE HELLENISTIC PERIOD 336–30 BC

The Persians never came back, but the Greeks always feared them as an enemy. In 334 BC, Alexander of **Macedonia** invaded the Persian Empire. He managed to defeat the Persians, and later became known as 'Alexander the Great'.

Alexander's generals soon fought and divided his empire into separate kingdoms, but those kingdoms kept their Greek character, spreading Greek culture and learning throughout the Middle East. This is known as the Hellenistic Period.

When parts of the Greek Empire were conquered by the Romans, many aspects of Greek life were absorbed into Roman culture. In this way, much of the scientific, artistic and cultural legacies of Greece have been passed down to western Europe.

A map showing the empire of Alexander. Greek art and learning dominated this entire area until the coming of the Romans and beyond.

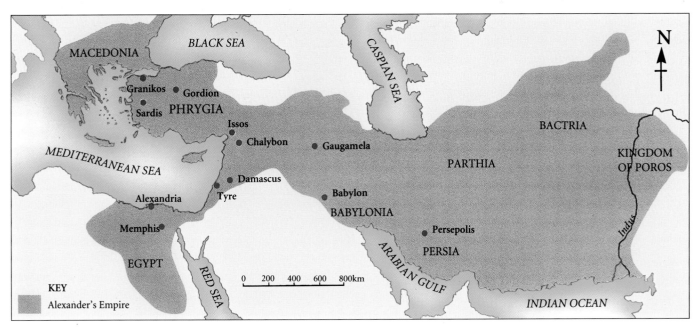

KEY

Alexander's Empire

GLOSSARY

Acropolis   This means 'high city' in Greek. It refers to a well-protected hill within a Greek city, where the main temples and sacred area were situated.

Agora   A market-place.

Andron   The dining room of a Greek house where men gave dinner parties for their male friends.

Aristocrats   Noble people.

Barbarian   This Greek word means 'foreigner'.

Berber   A person from north Africa in ancient Greek times.

City states   Cities plus the land and the villages around them.

Colonies   Territories that are outside the country which governs them.

Democracy   A system in which people can elect the government which they want.

Excavated   Dug up from the ground.

Famine   A time when there is very little food and many people starve.

Gynaeceum   A room in a Greek house, usually on the first floor, where the women and girls spent much of their time.

Hellene   The Greeks' name for themselves.

Hoplites   Well-armed Greek foot soldiers.

Macedonia   A kingdom to the north of Greece. Macedonian people thought of themselves as Greeks, although many did not accept them.

Mercenaries   Men paid to kill, or to fight for a foreign army.

Mosaic   A picture made from coloured pieces of paper, glass, stone or wood.

Mycenaean   This word comes from the leading city and kingdom in Greece, Mycenae, during an early period of Greek history.

Oligarchy   This means 'rule by the few' in Greek.

Pentathlon   An athletic contest in which each competitor takes part in five events. In the ancient Olympic Games this meant running, wrestling, jumping, and throwing the discus and the javelin.

Perioiloi   This means 'neighbours' in Greek. This was what the Spartans called the limited number of craftspeople and traders who were allowed to live in Sparta.

Phalanx   A unit of soldiers, drawn up close together. It was usually eight ranks deep.

Stoa   A columned walkway down the two long sides of a Greek market-place.

Strategos   In Athens, this was a military commander, who had powers to carry out the policies decided on by the Council and the Assembly. Athens had ten strategoi – one from each of the tribes into which Athenian men were grouped.

Tyrant   This meant ruler in ancient Greece. Today it means someone who rules cruelly or unfairly.

BOOKS TO READ

Burn, L. *Greek Myths* (British Museum Press, 1990)

Nichols, R. and McLeish, K. *Through Greek Eyes* (Cambridge University Press, 1991)

Nicholson, R. *Ancient Greece* (Two-Can Publishing, 1992)

Pearson, A. *What Do We Know About the Greeks?* (Simon and Schuster, 1992)

Steel, B. *Greek Cities* (Wayland, 1989)

Williams, A. S. *The Greeks* (Wayland, 1993)

PLACES TO VISIT

Ashmolean Museum, Beaumont Street, Oxford, OX1 2PH.
A fine collection of antiquities containing interesting Greek and Roman objects.

Birmingham City Museum, Chamberlain Square, Birmingham, B3 3DH.
A museum and gallery with a very good archaeology section, containing Greek objects.

British Museum, Great Russell Street, London WC1B 3DG.
The largest and finest collection of Greek antiquities in Britain.

Capesthorne Hall, Macclesfield, Cheshire SK11 9JY.
The house contains an important collection of Greek vases.

Fitzwilliam Museum, Trumpington Street, Cambridge CB2 1RB.
A museum which contains many fine ancient Greek works of art.

Greek Museum, University Department of Classics, Newcastle-upon-Tyne NE1 4XW.
This museum houses a fine collection of Athenian pottery, and a range of Greek weapons and armour.

If you visit Greece or the Greek islands on holiday, you will be able to visit the fine museums as well as the magnificent ruins. The south of Italy once had Greek colonies and has some important sites to visit.

INDEX